A WORLD WITHOUT COLOR

A TRUE STORY BY

BERNARD JAN

BERNARD JAN

A World Without Color

A True Story

by

Bernard Jan

Published by Bernard Jan, Zagreb, 2017

Originally published in Croatian as *Svijet bez boja* by Epifanija, Zagreb, 2008, ISBN 978-953-7077-08-2

www.bernardjan.com

Translated into English by Bernard Jan

Editing and proofreading by Philip Newey, Thomas Carley Jr. and Kath Middleton

Cover design by Mario Kožar MKM Media

Cover photo by Zach Singh

ISBN (Print On-Demand) 978-953-59581-1-6

Cataloguing-in-Publication data available in the Online Catalogue of the National and University Library in Zagreb under CIP record 000965244.

Contents

A WORLD WITHOUT COLOR

You curl up in your new hideout, and the soft light of the April afternoon washes your worn-out body. You are aware of my closeness. You confirm that with a gentle sigh while my palm tenderly slides down your fur. You still like my touch, although pain is what you now mostly feel. And uncertainty—but for how long?

Against the tracksuit pants I wipe a lock of your hair which is stuck to my palm. I try to take a better position, crawling next to you under the table. I hate the sentimentality of people who want to capture with photos the beautiful moments in life because they believe that's the only way they can remain part of their memories. Ironic, because I myself re-sort to this now. Nothing else is left for me. Another day, week, month at best is the most optimistic prognosis.

Only this time. I will make an exception.

Your chest is rising and falling, fighting for every breath. It's not easy for you, I know, and I would love most if I could breathe for you. But I can't. Even if I breathe a new life into you, it probably wouldn't help. You wouldn't even let me. Because you are a fighter. Besides, it seems to me you don't like people taking pity on you, as you didn't like it when they laughed in your face. This is why I control myself when I'm around you, poorly disguising the true nature of my feelings in a lame attempt to preserve your dignity. Panic hits me because of what is coming!

A tidal wave rushes from within, forcing tears to my eyes, which stream silently down my face and drip-drop onto your colorful blanket. Jolly green, purple and beige squares support your long, thin and distorted body like a gentle cloud. The shadow of what you used to be.

I support myself on my elbows, taking the first snapshot with my cell phone in my left hand. You hear a click and crack open your eyes. Your gaze rests on me, warming me with the heat of the hearth fire that fades away. I take another picture, producing another click, and then my hand trembles; I have to dry the tears that, undecided, stop and pause in the corners of my eyes.

You raise your head, not ceasing to look at me. Your good eye caresses my soul, while the other, sick from cataracts and inflammation unsuccessfully treated with ointments and drops, looks into the unknown. I'm stroking your hair, matted around it, waiting for you to be ready to continue our little photo session.

Again you accept me and indulge my whim. Gently as a newborn, you push your head along my hand, responding to my caress. First you rub your little nose into my fingers, and then you push your left ear against my hand, wanting me to scratch and massage it. When you become bored or you think it is enough, with amazing vigor you start to wash yourself. You surprise me a little because I don't remember when was the last time I saw you wash yourself. (It was a long time ago, just as eons have gone by since the days when you would happily nestle in the most comfortable seat in the apartment, after successfully sponging an abundant meal, and start to clean yourself. An invisible clock, or timer in you—as we used to joke—woke you up and led you, with your tail raised, to your bowls, where you patiently waited until, usually Mom, capitulated before your determination and persistence of the winner.) I smile, encouraged by a false hope and strong mental images awakened from the past. How little it takes for the Phoenix to resurrect in me and clatter the wings of joy. How dishonest I am with myself (and you) and subject to self-deception!

I leave you for a moment and hurry into the kitchen to show the photos to Mom. You continue sprucing up, as you know it's time for Saša's arrival. As always, you want to show yourself to him in the best light. You care about what Saša thinks of you. I don't think you do this so he can pet you and lavish words of praise on you, calling you *Viola, Love.* No, you accept Saša because you know you will be better each time you see him and you want to give something back to him. You want to show him that his visits really make you feel better. And so you do that. I don't know with which words I can express more clearly what I feel for you, so I will repeat: *Viola, my love.*

My thoughts come rushing back like raging currents of mountain rivers that do not stop for anything or anyone. Hurrying with a roar to their finish line, completely self-sufficient. Each word I make immortal here must be engraved with the dedication of a blind stonemason who, just by sense of touch and guided by indestructible faith, creates from the shapeless mass a work which present generations, but also those who come after, will admire. Those who are alive today, and their children who are just born, setting the foundation for new generations. This is our written monument and I snuggle up against it, blinded by the pain inflicted upon me by every minute that takes us into the future. The future is what I want to avoid at any cost, selfishly keeping the present so these moments last as long as possible. Not thinking about you and the relief it will bring you. We are both on the road of no return. Do you think so too? Do you also feel at least a fraction of regret we will part soon, with no guarantee and no promise that, in the blink of an eye or the distant future, we might meet each other again? Tell me, dearest....

Tonight, I am watching over you. I leave the desk lamp on, wishing to better guard over the timid work of your lungs from which the rattles and squeals of suffocation no longer emerge after Saša has given you the injections. One could see how you livened up and hurried to the bowl to satisfy your thirst with the very diluted milk. You wanted to boast to Saša that you were doing better and let him know how much his visits mean to you and how much you appreciate what he does for you. If only you knew how proud I am of you!

Your regular breathing lulls me to sleep, from which

I awake unaccustomed to the neon light transforming the night in our room into a polar day. I fall to sleep again and twitch, awakened by the beeping of the electric doors of the late-night trams, the roaring engines of occasional cars that chase the empty street, and even rarer passers-by, to whom the nightlife is nothing more alien than that illuminated by daylight. They are both the children of the moon and the children of the sun; unlike me, who always favors the heat of the sun over the beauty of the night sky dotted with myriads of distant stars.

I doze off and miss when you get up and pause to gather strength before undertaking the long journey down the hall to the living room where your bowls are waiting for you under the window. Still sleepy, I subconsciously hear Saša's words: if you know the routes of his movement, carry him there so he doesn't get tired. I jump headlong into my slippers and stumble after you. I have to be careful not to wake Mom and Dad who sleep in the furthest room next to the bathroom. A small corridor separates it from the living room, the same one which connects the living room with the kitchen, pantry and the maid's room. I put one of my hands under your chest while the other I place under your hind legs, lifting you up as light as a feather and carrying you to your refreshments.

It's still not midnight, I see by the big, mercury-gray wall clock, which we received as a gift from the bookkeeping service where I worked for three years before I turned that page in life and became fully active in the animal protection and rights association. Having enough of the diluted milk from the right half of the bowl you switch to the left one which also contains diluted milk. You make strange gurgling and belching noises while drinking, resting to regain your breath. Again you fight the battle with the body which does not give up, though experiencing defeat after defeat. The desire to heal it and keep it in force is stronger than the pain it causes you, stronger than common sense. Your legs are shaking and weak while they carry you to a bowl with water and crackers, only a two-step process. You wheeze and catch your breath, but you don't give up. You drink. Water is like antibiotics to you, and when you're done here, you will go back to the saucer to the right of the bowl with milk where acidophilus awaits you. You refresh yourself with it. Then you raise your eyes to me in the dark and expectantly, and I know what I must do. Some four hours ago Saša relieved your bladder by squeezing it. It is not pee time yet. So I take you in my arms as a snowflake and carry you back to your bed.

I kneel to lower you down as gently as possible and make it easier for you to land on your unnaturally elongated and weakened hind legs. Awkwardly stepping on them and swaying, you crawl under the table. I follow you, crawling on my knees. I cuddle you and calm you until your breathing is normalized, and then I slip under the quilt on my floor bed. Listening to whether your breathing will again become shrill, I fall asleep without even being aware of it.

The next time I wake up on time. About an hour has passed, and you wait for me to take you in my arms and carry you to the bowls with food. No problem, love.

Tonight I'm yours. Count on me. When you're done, I carry you to the corridor between the kitchen, pantry, children's and living room, where three boxes make up your small bathroom. A pile of newspaper is spread below them. I lower you into the nearest box, with fresh kitty litter covered with three layers of paper towels. My slippers rustle through the papers, under which is ammonia-eaten and bleached parquet—a consequence of your slumbering and belated attempts to get to the toilet. So as not to wake my parents, I close the door to the corridor in front of their room. I listen. Hearing quiet snoring from a dark room, I give in to your stubbornness. I take you back under the table with unfinished business. It's the night. I'm tired and have no energy—or heart—to fight against your character and will. That's what I appreciate about you. You don't allow yourself to be bossed around and you do things in your own time, reminding me of myself! I wait until your breathing calms again, and then I crawl into bed too.

Mom wakes up just before seven o'clock, groggy and with trepidation about whether this morning she will also find wet newspaper and more eaten parquet. By the time she is up, we have repeated your nightly ritual five more times. The last time I lay in bed a little after six o'clock, long ago having turned off the desk lamp, accompanied by the dawn that pressed through the windows with open curtains and lifted blinds. Fatigue crawls through my body, and I catch the last hour of an illusory dream before facing the challenge of a new day.

I hate working days that are made into holidays! It gets on my nerves when everything stops, when nothing is open and you have no place to go, and well-wishers, who spent the whole day devouring the bodies of tortured and slaughtered animals, occupy our phone. The words *I wish you happy this, happy that* are frustrating, human hypocrisy that sees no further than its own stomach. There are the days when I feel like one of them—a hypocrite—when I am not persistent enough, stubborn and determined enough, to reason with my old folks and talk them out of buying slaughtered chickens for you. If you only knew your food was coming from these mistreated creatures who spend their miserable lives crammed in cages where they cannot spread their wings, and peck each other from stress and frustration, I'm sure you would boycott it too. Alone I was too weak to fight the windmills, and your being sick and being eaten up by diabetes certainly did not go in my favor.

Don't worry. I don't blame you for anything. You are made the way you are made, and nobody can blame you for that. But we, humans, have a choice: the choice between good and evil, compassion and cruelty, empathy and ignoring, and we do not use it. We do not use common sense because our stomach blinds our mind and everything flows through it. At least most of us.

Ah....

What now flows through my stomach are new spasms caused by crying. Again I succumb to my emotions and tears blind my vision as a summer shower blocks the view through the windshield of the car at full speed. Nice memories of the days we spent together arise in me, only to be nibbled by the sour taste of reality.

One moment I see you alive and playful, in pursuit of a ball of aluminum foil that is rolling and sliding on the parquet while you chase it with your little paws around the apartment in the never-ending game; the next moment I see you dejected and curled up in a cardboard box, in search of peace and solitude. Then, without a break, I see you jumping after the piece of string I hold in my hand while we all laugh at your acrobatics; and a moment later I see you lying on the carpet next to the armchair I sit in, too weak and too sick to jump into my lap and settle down there. The high tides and ebb tides of feelings turn in me faster than those caused by the magical allure of the moon, crushing me and grinding me into the granules of the person I am becoming, while salty sea water withdraws from the coasts, sprinkled with the fine sand of oblivion.

Yesterday we had a serious talk with Saša about the possibility of putting you down. We have not talked to you about that, but somehow I feel you foresee it, that you have exposed us and that nothing remains hidden from you. You read all around you like X-rays, and stoically, calmly and gracefully handle what is coming. I wish I could be brave like you and look death in the face with equal force and dignity. The hopelessness of your nonexistence, which covers me like a magician's cloak, prevents me from that. Stealing me, stealing you. *I do not agree to such a deal!* As long as there is a fire in you for one more battle, as long as *you* do not say it's over.

Absently I wipe my tears and take a book, leaving you to rest. King's horror stories go past me, but I do not experience them. Have I become immune to fear? Have I become immune to everything around me, whether fictional or real? *Why do you hurt me so much then?!*

Putting aside the book I furtively take a bunch of wet handkerchiefs and throw them in the washing machine. From the closet in my grandma's room I take clean handkerchiefs and blow my nose. I return to you and check up on you; instead of checking my e-mails and updating the website with translated texts, I reach out again for King's *Nightmares & Dreamscapes*. Today I'm not capable of anything which requires my concentration. I can't think about work now. Even if an asteroid crashed into the earth and caused a new ice age, I wouldn't care the least. Today I breathe and live for you. So I can give you some of my life energy; so I can take at least part of your pain. Both unsuccessfully.

Therapy with horror-stories doesn't work—not one story gets a hold of me; the reality is more frightening than any fictional story. Again you get up and, pausing, continue on your way to drink some milk. Better to say lots of milk because since you were diagnosed with diabetes four years ago you drink a great deal. The knocking sound of your bones on the floor blends with Mom's voice. I hear her babble to you. You spread love and good vibrations wherever you appear as you have all these fourteen years and nine months. I don't know about you, but if someone gives us as much time as a gift, it won't be enough for me. On second thoughts, you are the best thing that ever happened to me. Thanks to you I could survive the dementia, illness and death of my grandmother, who vegetated for years before she found her deserved peace. Thanks to you I managed to cope every day with atrocious images of animals raised and slaughtered for human consumption, massacred in laboratory experiments, skinned for their fur... or those unwanted and discarded before they were run over on the roads. You were one of them too—discarded. Unwanted. One of those sentenced to death immediately after birth. Luck has smiled on you in the end. If I'm to be honest, luck favored us. Many times I thought: if it wasn't for you, this family might have already gone to hell. But you keep us together. As the gravity of the home planet holds its satellites, not allowing them to wander into the universe of the unknown. If you, my star, die out, I don't know what will happen to this constellation called your family. Maybe everything will be fine, despite my black prognosis, and maybe not. Maybe the memory of you will bring us even closer and keep us from falling apart like dried clay. I can't think about that now. Every moment we have left, every breath I take, I want to give to you. This is what I owe you. It's the least I can do for you. That is what I want.

You're coming back with lowered and plump belly (your abdomen is the only thing on you that still looks like in the days when you were healthy and full of life) and buckling legs. Stopping under the chair for a second or two, you carry on to your blanket. The routine which you do not give up brings back a pale smile to my face and dispels the darkness that swallows me. You are here, you exist beside me, and I am grateful for your life. Perhaps you cannot understand that (and maybe you're not the only one who will not understand), but your existence gives meaning to my life. You represent what is worthy and should be fought for: you are the symbol of incorruptibility, benevolence, innocence, purity, kindness, sincerity, selflessness, goodness, friendship, and love, qualities that should inhabit every corner of this planet. If we were all like you, we wouldn't need redemption. Nor would we need to sacrifice and kill others for our sins. The world would be the way it was supposed to be, and not this muddy, dirty and bloody quagmire wrapped in a false cellophane, in which we wallow day after day. Full of illusions and running away from the truth!

We are lying next to each other; not even six and a half feet separate us. Each of us in his own thoughts, chained by our fears and tortured by our own pain. But here we are, together, as we were at the time of the rocket attacks on Zagreb when you were still a baby, and when I didn't want to leave you alone in the apartment while the air was screaming with a siren alarm. We were both scared then. Although it was a little over fourteen years ago, I remember well your unrest and your big, round, yellow-green eyes, further enlarged by fear. I remember when you purred when I sat next to you on a two-seater in the living room (which we have, in the meantime, replaced with a three-seater) and took you in my lap. You were never one of those cats who purred loud and often; actually, you purred rather quietly, shyly and rarely. And you meowed rarely, talking to us. But at that moment you rejected your restraint and presented me with a few soothing and timeless moments in nights filled with uncertainty, hostility, fear and the flame of candles.

As if it was encoded in your genes, you hated to travel by car, so we took you only a few times to the unknown environment of our cottage. During the ride, you would take revenge on us by throwing up and doing the big business in the car which prompted us to open the windows in a hurry. You therefore spent most of your time with us in the apartment, showing yourself as a worthy, fearless and skilled hunter, as were your ancestors and brothers. If I recall well, on two occasions Mom had to remove from your little jaws stiff and scared sparrows you caught on the balcony. Your walk on the thin railing, beyond which was a yawning chasm to the concrete courtyard sixty-five feet below, chilled our blood! Even now I'm shaking from the thought of what would have happened if you slipped, and what would be left of you if your twenty-two pounds—what you weighed back then—began to plunge. How many years of life you took from us then, and yet you are the one who is leaving before us all....

Your feline instinct didn't prevent you, regardless of the fear of the unknown and undiscovered world, from jumping from the terrace of the cottage and slipping away into the garden. I panicked that, guided by the call of nature and curiosity that has killed so many cats, you would squeeze under the fence and irrevocably and forever disappear into the wild. I ran after you like crazy, almost jumping from the terrace myself, pulled you from under the cypress tree planted right next to the fence and firmly held you against my chest. Two hearts pounded against each other, both in fear of what could be or what would happen. You, fearing punishment that did not come, and I terrified by the vision of the loss that had not occurred. I wasn't indifferent when, the next morning, Mom told me you were waiting at the door before the church bell finished ringing and took her for a walk through the wet grass, bathed in dew, over which fog was still lazily dozing. You took her for an early morning walk, step by step, carefully lifting your paws and lowering them in a small, private world teeming with life and creatures you knew only from the heritage transferred from your father and mother and their fathers and mothers, and that you didn't know personally. Mom followed you, shivering and still half-asleep, in a chilly rural morning, taking care of you, of your every step. You prowled, smelled the air and the ground, moved whiskers and raised your head, belly wet and kept flat with the grass, steering your tail and transmitting strange signals with it. It was your conquest. It was a time of youth and research expeditions. It was a time of joy, laughter; but also fear that the gods of nature would grab you in your quest. The fear of losing you was omnipresent. I couldn't resist it because I rather possessively loved you and cared for you. Because I took responsibility when I brought you home. The moment I took you in my arms, when I felt life breathing on the palm of my hand in the shape of a small, furry ball shaking with shock and uncertainty, I realized the enormity of the world and the love that brought us into existence.

You were small. You lay in my hand and I could have crushed you if I squeezed my palm a little harder—and you were larger than life. In that moment, in those first few minutes before I gave you to Mom, I felt the power of nature, the power of the divine and driving forces of the world, the magnificent universe that provides us a home and the monumentality of a responsibility I took with you. I knew I would stay with you until the end, that we would spend life together. Then I didn't know when and how the end would come. Nor who would be the first to say *it's over*. Encyclopedias of nice images have been written since then, enriched with beautiful photographs of warm and cheerful colors. While the last pages are being written and the cover of the last volume slowly being closed, the fear from which I was suffering then now seems so benign and ridiculous.

I agree and swear on another double and triple the dose, only to stop the inevitable! I agree and swear on all the joys and sorrows, all the uncertainties, my bloody hands and your claws stuck in my arms and legs, only to delay what you are telling me with your every look. I see you are saying goodbye. You are the one who will first take another road, leaving us in chains of sorrow, to wait, believe and hope that we will once again meet. In a world with no promises, in a world which by the hour seems more alien and less the home to which I belong.

If there is such a thing as *déja vu*, now I need it more than ever. I invoke it. I pray for a break in the repeating of what has already happened. The reason wants to move on, but feelings do not want to unmoor and sail away without you into a new world. It's hard.... And I'm afraid it will be even harder.

I'm breaking down.

I'm breaking down—that is a concept, that is a word, that is a construction of words which acquires a different and, for me, clearer meaning. I am not a cracked branch of a tree, which breaks off from its source of life, nor am I a broken nail that was chipped due to negligence, and has then fallen off. But the pain that accompanies a broken-off nail is the pain I feel while I'm breaking down. In myself, in the silence of my being, without a scream or any visible sign but tears.

My love, if you go away in a few days, the world will lose its colors and darken like the land of Mordor. If you go away and leave me to wander aimlessly, alone in this sea become wild, like a ship with a broken rudder and drowned sailors, and if I don't find comfort in the warmth of your body, clutched in my embrace at the end of the day, I'm afraid I won't survive. I'm not afraid of waters and I am not a non-swimmer, but foam and wind could suffocate me before I swim up to you—my shore, solid ground. Allow me to love you a little longer and breathe a few more times before I realize I must carry on alone. You won your victory; the hardest battle is still in front of me.

I don't turn the pages anymore, but count the hours in anticipation of Saša's arrival. I hope that yesterday you didn't notice the shock in his eyes when he saw you and gently told you *Viola*. I could not say how it happened, but then everything was already decided. We won't be able to wait for you to leave by yourself; we will have to help you in this.

Euthanasia and *putting down* are the words I avoid most these days. To the extent that I don't want to admit they exist and snapped at Luka and Snježana when they told me we are torturing you by keeping you alive like this. I was determined that we will give you medication therapy as long as you show even the smallest willingness to fight for your life.

I regret that I went that day to the association (usually it is not difficult for me to work on a holiday) to catch up with some of the backlog that piled up to the sky, all from our burning desire and enthusiasm to help so many animals. Now it seems to me that I have not helped them at all, and that I stole from you a few precious hours we could have spent together.

They weren't ill-intentioned when they said that. After all, Jelena e-mailed me too that she could never let you suffer so much. Maja, who also was in the office and who affectionately called you *pee-pee* because of your habit of peeing on our parquet (this is why she collected and sent you newspapers after we cut out the articles we needed for our archive), also worried about you. But how could I explain to them, how could I explain to anyone, how much you mean to me?! Your presence in my life is like a room filled with lamps. When you're gone, the brightest, the prettiest one will go out. And leave behind the half-light of unclear shadows.

I agree that no form of addiction is good. I know it only too well. However, disappointed in people and the world in which I must exist, I was unwary when I became attached to you. It didn't happen overnight. It was a lengthy process, and therefore the trap was more hidden. But the addiction therefore became stronger! I don't care how people will characterize me: a lunatic or a sick person. I don't care about the opinion of *such* people. But I care about you, as I would care about my brother if I had the chance to get to know him—an immediate family member, or a loyal friend to whom this faithless world gave birth. Sticks and stones may break my bones, but their words won't hurt me. What I'm not sure about, but would like to know, is if I have been at least half as faithful to you as you have been faithful to me. Will you forgive me the moments I have devoted to others, which were rightly yours?

Tonight Saša injected a new dose of hope into me. I almost cried with relief and joy when I was in the bathroom above the sink, holding you by your front legs, and Saša was gently and patiently squeezing your bladder from behind. I have to admit it was a funny situation! First you meowed in protest, but then you purred loudly from relief. You purred so strongly that I felt vibrations in my fingers! I was tempted to kiss you, but we were in the midst of more important business. When I put you down on your foam-like soft pillow, where joyful puppies smiled, slept and played, you did not move, but remained lying as I placed you. You only sank into it, forgetting at least for a moment about the pain that tortured your body. Your face was radiant with pleasure, and your good eye followed us while we escorted Saša to the door. Bye, love, see you tomorrow, he told you on leaving. Luckily for you and unfortunately for me, but I didn't know that then.

Night is falling, and I am getting ready for another vigil. With Mom and Dad I again consider putting the box where you can sleep next to your food so you would not have to take the trouble of going back and forth. I am even thinking about moving onto a three-seater in the living room to sleep next to you. My idea is not well received because you decide to sleep under the table in my room, and, even before, while your box was there, you would not sleep in it. Therefore, I go earlier to bed today so I have the strength to stay awake with you. But I can't sleep. Since I don't have the habit of going to bed before eleven o'clock—if I lose track of time reading a book I will even go to sleep about one in the morning— my biorhythm is playing games with me and there's no way that, in spite of being tired, I can fall asleep. I end up in an armchair in front of a mind-numbing television program on Monday evening.

Tonight, also, we go for our first walk just before midnight. You drag yourself from your shelter under the table and wait for me to open my eyes and lift you in my arms. Obediently and quietly I carry you to your bowls and, in the dark, watch how you alternately drink water and diluted milk. Your hind legs awkwardly shape a letter L tucked under you, and with every few new sips your tummy becomes a little bigger. Your ribs spookily stick out of your sides, emphasizing the emptiness you have turned into between your spine and pelvic bones. The bones of your hind legs protrude from it sharply, covered with a thin layer of skin and rare hair, corroded by urine. That gets me thinking again whether the milk you drank sped up your deterioration because cow's milk draws calcium from the bones instead of enriching them. But you want to drink only milk, even if so diluted that it tastes like water flavored with milk. Water is your last choice, which you don't fancy much. I understand. We all have our little desires which we are not willing to give up, so I do not make a big deal out of it, nor have I prevented you from drinking. Even if I did, what would I achieve? Your way and destination are already known. It is only a question of time.

Happy that tonight you don't make disturbing

noises, as you did the previous night, I carefully lift you up. Your swollen tummy warms the wrist of my right hand while I carry you to your bed. I cuddle you and tell you to sleep, and I do the same. Another walk begins about an hour later, and then you eat a few dietary crackers. The situation from last night—you scared me when your front right leg twisted so much that it turned into a distorted letter O—does not repeat. Actually, it was more like a frightening combination of the letter O and the letter S. You shook it, tried to stand on it, but it buckled under you each time and you stumbled, almost diving with your nose into a bowl of crackers. I tried to help you by supporting you, but I grabbed you clumsily and you started to choke. I carried you to the three-seater and laid you down on your pillow. It was about three in the morning. I sat next to you and stroked your bad leg with my hand, and you laid it on the index finger of my left hand and left it there while I kept stroking you. I was breaking down, watching you like this. Precious, meek, humble, cuddly, and suave. Pretty, despite the illness that turned your once beautiful, gray-brown fur, rich with tiger stripes, into several shades of brown fur which has lost its stripes, and got dandruff instead. When you lifted your leg off my finger, I walked barefoot back to my room to retrieve my blanket, for I was cold. I cuddled next to you, wrapped in the blanket, still keeping an eye on you. About five to seven minutes went by and your little head dropped. It was getting heavier and heavier and inch by inch lowered itself to the pillow until it sank into it. You were sleeping, and I continued to guard over you.

I wondered what you dreamed. Did you have a peaceful sleep or did you feel pain even while dreaming? Your legs and body didn't twitch as they usually did when you were chasing someone in a dream. I wondered, how it was to hunt in a dream and then wake up aware that you could not run, let alone hunt someone? How did it feel... to wake up and stand on weak legs which produced thuds as you clumsily walked on parquet and carpet? With effort, but determined to carry you from one end of the apartment to another.

Sometimes I would love to penetrate your thoughts and find out what is going on in your head, instead of reading from your eyes and facial expressions how strong is the current of your love for us. Or what you really think, how you feel about us. Mom is the one who mainly feeds you and cleans up after you; Dad's responsibility is to give you his healing energy by stroking you with the sole of his foot. Sometimes you sponge something from him. You come to me when you're in the mood for cuddling, and you wait for me in my room when I'm coming home. This room has become your permanent residence in the last few days. I would like to better communicate with you, but my limited body and mind prevent me. I would like to know how cats function and what you talk about when you meet. Do you have the same quarrels as we, stupid people, or do you communicate in a more sophisticated and humane way?

For almost forty minutes I sit next to you, not ceasing to think. If Mom only knew her wish will soon come true! More than once she has pestered me to write something about you, but I wonder if she had this in mind when she asked me. It was long ago when she last mentioned it. Then you were still in full strength and full of adventures you repeated as in child's play. What comes clearest to mind is when you, so tiny, ran under the two-seater, and we couldn't get you out until you mustered courage to come out by yourself; or when you forced Dad and me to move the two-seater so Mom could catch you. And when you became too big to crawl under it, you hid between the two-seater and the wall, and Mom and I, each from one side of the two-seater, called you and tried to lure you out. Not to mention how you liked to crawl in closets and a chest for bedding, especially during the winter! Besides being warmer there, hiding in closets and other hidden places gave you special satisfaction. Things have changed since then. We all have changed. Only what we feel for each other remains the same. We for you and you for us. The only thing that has remained stable and strengthened with time.

I adjusted the cloth with which we cover you during the cold winter days because you no longer have strength to warm yourself. It's too late now. I will never get those answers. If you die on me, if you leave me, I don't think I will have another animal. Now I understand my mom when she said not in a million years would she have another cat after Fanika's death. I didn't understand her. I didn't listen to her, and I didn't respect her decision. This is not my punishment, but now I will find out too in the cruelest and most painful way what she meant when she said *never again*. All right, I won't go that far and say never again; but chances are high you are my first, last and only animal. Adopting someone after you, after all we've been through together, seems like a betrayal. Like the desecration of everything beautiful we had. And that was in abundance. I wouldn't trade the time we had for all the wonders of this world.

It is interesting that you too accepted us as your family more than you accepted other animals. I remember well your running away from Micka, uncle's cat, when we brought her to socialize with you. It was chaos, and I thought you two would pluck each other's eyes out. You needed five years to stop hiding from the people who visited us, to trust and approach them, whether you already knew them or they were complete strangers to you. For years you've felt the trauma you experienced when you were born, when savage young brats from Zagreb's Peščenica poured water over you until Sonja, a friend of the family, rescued you and brought you as my present for Mom's birthday. (It was a perfect excuse for me to finally get a cat!) God, you were so tiny when I brought you wrapped up in a cloth to our apartment and showed you to my parents! Mom was gaping in amazement and disbelief, thinking I was joking, while my old man almost went crazy with worry about his allergy to cat hair. (Yeah right! Later it turned out that this was his perfect excuse for me *not* to get a cat!) For two months he kept asking when Sonja would return for you. (It was a story we sold him—that Sonja had to temporarily home you with us because of her cat, but that she would come back for you—playing the card that over time he would get used to you so he wouldn't give you away.) In the end he was so fond of you that every fifteen minutes or less he went to see what Pipo was doing. Yes, it's not a joke. They gave you that stupid nickname after food you liked to eat before you had to switch your diet to crackers for diabetics.

Do you remember, my old buddy, how you attacked Mom if she wouldn't give you food when your programmed timer signaled it was feeding time? When she left you waiting too long, or she didn't please you because you were overweight? You ambushed her and then grabbed her legs and arms! A real little rascal! It's hard for me to connect the image of you playful and full of energy with what I see now: you so weak, scrawny and fragile, a pale copy of what you used to be. As if it isn't you! I will tell you a secret though. The older and more powerless you became, the stronger my feelings for you grew. No, my precious, you didn't come to a family which gets rid of the helpless when they grow old and cannot entertain them any longer, or whatever. You hit the jackpot because this family is not ready to give up on you. We will fight for you no matter what, no matter how much it costs us—financially and emotionally. You were lucky you didn't come among egomaniacs who throw their pets onto the street when they are no longer interesting to them. You have come to your *home*. You are no longer an abandoned and unwanted creature, but a full member of the family, with all its rights and privileges. You are *loved*.

Suddenly you raised your head, waking up in a flash. As if all this time you were faking it and listening to my thoughts. I unwrapped myself from the blanket and once more carried you to your bowls. This time your legs held you. Forty-five minutes of rest helped.

I have to admit, these abrupt reversals of the situation, when your legs can't support you and you can't stand on them, rather confuse me. They awake and kill hope in me, and I don't know what to think. For example, when I returned on Saturday from our regular info stall, the weather was beautiful. Even before I got home, I decided that I would take you out to the balcony so you could enjoy the sun and fresh breeze. But when I took you in my arms and sat with you on the balcony threshold, you were so calm and disinterested that even the pigeon, The Winged, wasn't afraid of you but kept watching us from the railing. I thought you'd enjoy that moment, but you surrendered to my will, lying in my lap like a rag puppet. You stretched your long legs while I could count all your vertebrae just by feeling them; they pressed so much into the arm you were leaning on. I cleaned us both of your hair that was shed and fluttered around us and brought you back under the table. While I was making more comfortable accommodation for you, I locked eyes with the pigeon, The Winged. (My old folks called him that because one of his lowered wings looked as it was broken.) Leg to leg he moved on the railing and stretched his neck, peeking into the room to see what we were doing. It was one of the defeats that shook me. A bell rang a silent alarm in me. You are not well, love, you are really not well.

When you get up for the third time to quench your thirst, you are faster than me. Overcome by the vigil and exhaustion I had fallen asleep, and catch up with you only when you have already reached your bowls, scratching with your nails on the floor. This time I can't persuade you to take a pee, as at two and then three in the morning. Your bladder has widened and become rounded again, but in the dead of night I can't do much about it so I carry you back to sleep. A similar thing happens at four o'clock and then again at quarter past five. Waking up after five, you visit Mom's pots in search of a little greenery and eat her asparagus. I must give you credit for your fight with time and your body, and the love for life you show in every step. You have not surrendered even though you've lost most of your teeth (it had to be a shock to you), but you relentlessly crush crackers with your gums, pull grass and swallow pieces of white chicken meat that Mom and Dad, in spite of my protests, still serve you.

I feel great relief when you finally urinate after six o'clock. Both last night and tonight you got up seven times (and me together with you). You drank long and a lot (for two and three minutes), and only two times you went to pee. I'm sorry I counted and monitored your every step, but I had to for your own good. Mom tells me you peed two more times between the time she got up (at seven o'clock) and I came out of the bathroom (around eight-fifteen). On both occasions you didn't even wet the newspaper with which we covered the entire hallway and part of the living room next to it—including the parquet which we rarely managed to protect with newspaper or nylon, no matter how hard we tried and how clever we were—where your toilets are.

A new day promises a lot. Since both of us spent the night more or less okay (excluding the fact that you were still in pain and still suffocating, but less than before, and that I was groggy from lack of sleep), I leave the house in a relatively cheerful mood. I expect a pile of work will be waiting for me in the office, but after the regular checking of e-mails and paying bills with online banking, I am lucky to spend the second half of the day driving with Luka and Maja from a mechanic to the store with vegan products, visiting the printing office to see the proof copy of the brochure against animal experiments and going to the bookkeeper for a statistical report. Everything hints that the day will end calmly and well, until, somewhere around half past six, I come home. Then my world turns upside down.

*

Saša is sitting by your head. Mom is behind your back, while Dad is standing in the middle of the room, red in face, his eyes wet with tears. They don't have to say anything for me to understand what is going on. It is not good. You are very sick. You choked the whole day. They think it no longer makes sense to torment you.

I drop the backpack next to the locker for shoes that stands between the living room door and my (sorry, our) room, take off Geoff Rowley vegan sneakers and fish cell phones from the pockets of my pants.

Is it that bad? I ask and get from Saša a brief but clear description of your condition. When he came to see you on Monday, he was taken aback by how much you had deteriorated in the two days he was away during the holidays. He didn't tell us then because he wanted to treat you with the injection therapies. He hoped to prolong your life for a few days, weeks, months…. But the improvement that had occurred due to the injections was only temporary and your condition has deteriorated again. He strokes your head while you breathe, relaxed, calm, with your mouth slightly open.

You are better because you have received an injection of painkillers, Mom adds, but what if you die during the night? We all struggle with ourselves and our feelings, Mom, Dad, Saša and me, knowing what is the right decision, but still postponing it. As if we expect a last-minute miracle.

I don't want to rush you, Saša continues. Think about everything overnight, but, if you want, I can do it today. His words sink in. Tired from lack of sleep, crying and under invasion of all kinds of thoughts and memories that besieged me during these last three days as you grew worse, I realize what Saša is saying.

You can do it now? I blurt out while my voice gains and loses its strength like a failing sound system.

I can do it tonight. I just need to get back to the clinic to pick up injections because I didn't bring them with me. I thought we would treat him, but all this has become a great burden and torture for him.

You could really do that? Mom looks at me, asking for confirmation. Dad wants to jump out of his skin.

There's no problem at all. I will be back in fifteen, twenty minutes tops.

And then you will take him with you? It seems Mom wants to have everything covered.

Yes, I will take him with me....

To the incinerator, I add.

I've been thinking about burying you in the backyard of our cottage in Zagorje, but I'm obviously not too fond of that idea or I would speak in favor of it now. Everything seems complicated. I don't know how we would drive you there because both Dad and I would be incapable of driving; and that place doesn't mean much to you because you visited it only a few times and you were stressed about it (apart from your morning expeditions and quests with Mom and jumps from the terrace after which I was running after you all over the yard). Your home is here, in this apartment. Since you can't stay here, it isn't so important where you will end up. Don't you think so too? *Am I at least a little right???*

But how will you take him? Aren't you on foot? I ask Saša. You're not thinking of carrying him on the tram?

I'm going home toward Dubrava, anyway. When I

get home, I'll bring the car and drive him. You prepare a bag for me so I can carry him in something. The rest is my concern.

And cloths. We will put him in the cloths he slept on and with which we covered him. I continue this morbid dialogue in front of you. I can't understand how one can have such a bizarre conversation at the time of extinguishing one life, when you are about to kill your favorite person.

You watch and listen to all that, silent and struggling for each breath. Calm and majestic, like the sphinx, the pride of the pharaohs. You still care little about what's going on around you, as if you have also made the same decision.

Stroking you again, Saša gets up.

Maybe I'll ask a colleague with the car to take him there, he says, remembering this possibility.

Thank you very much, Saša. You helped us a lot. I don't know how we would do this without you, Mom says.

It's nothing, please. I know how you feel. It's not easy for me either. The two of us bonded and I think it is okay if I do it. I could send someone else to do it for me, but it wouldn't be fair to him....

Once more he confirms that he will be back soon, and then he puts on his jacket and leaves. Bitter is the trace left in us as the door closes behind him.

This was approximately how our conversation went before the countdown of the last minutes you will spend with us, in your family. I say approximately, for I cannot claim with certainty who said what in these very emotional moments. But I think I have pretty well reconstructed what happened, with small omissions. It is true that, since I came home, I haven't been in control of my body, mind and, least of all, feelings. I change my T-shirt, but I keep on the pants I wore to work—I don't know why. I use the opportunity of being alone and quickly wipe my eyes and blow my nose. I don't want you to see me like this, neither you nor my parents. I have to be strong, for you—so you can go surrounded by love and gratitude, and not tears and lamentations, but also for Mom and Dad—to give them strength with my calmness to get through this hard, hard day. The hardest day of my life, and I'm not ashamed to admit that.

It is a long and, at the same time, such a short twenty minutes. I sit beside you while you lie on your soft pillow, barely responding to my caress. As if you are entirely focused on your breathing, on each new breath that will prolong your life a little. You resemble more the breathing apparatus than the person with whom I have spent almost fifteen years of life, which can't be redeemed by all the treasures of this world.

Mom is also sitting next to you and strokes you, repeating how this is the best for you, assuring you that our kitty will find his peace now, and that nothing will hurt you where you are going.

I don't know who came up with the idea to shoot a

few last photos as a memento. Maybe it was me. It doesn't matter now. It was one thing saying that and quite another doing it. Mom and Dad try to explain to me, distracted as I am by being nervous, how the camera works, but I can't shoot one photo of you! Frustrated, I give the camera to Mom. And Mom, and Dad after her, take a few pictures of you without a problem. Only later, six days after you are already dead, when we develop the film, it will be obvious they weren't too successful either. Only seven of them will be good; others will turn out blurred and smeared, like too-diluted watercolor on wrinkled rice paper.

I leave Mom alone with you for a minute. To stay strong and brave, I need to remove the tears that escape unnoticed, and to handle the sobs that torture me. Watching the street, I see the people and the windows of the surrounding buildings. At one of the open windows stands a couple smoking. In others the lights are on. It is dark in my room, and that same darkness creeps into me too.

Conversation with Mom consists of rare and short sentences which quickly fade from my memory. You are the one big thought that fills my whole mind. No matter how hard I try to be a rock, the more I stumble against desperation and cognition that fill me as a roaring torrent filling an empty tank with water. I won't hear you again, tapping with your feet while coming out of my room, pausing in the hallway and peeking behind a cabinet for shoes. You would scan the room where the three of us sat, gathered in front of the TV, me usually holding a book. Then, encouraged by my words—*and whom do I see there*—you marched to your bowls with pride and the graciousness of a leopard and, in spite of your illness, ignoring us all.

In the morning you won't come to my room, sprawl under the table while the radio is playing, and I am getting ready for work. You loved music, and every time I turned the radio on or played something from a CD, you would relax and go to sleep in the blink of an eye. Music was like anesthetic to you and I'm sorry there

50

won't be music where you are going. I'm sorry I didn't see you off with music....

Nor will I any longer come home and be greeted by you under the table as if you hadn't moved from there since I went out. Mom tells me you would lie on the pillow in the living room, and a few minutes before I rang downstairs you would move to my room and lie under the table. You knew I would be home any minute. You felt that. I do not doubt that as I do not doubt that a void will come into your place and swallow me day by day like death swallowed our relationship.

No longer will you jump into my lap while I sit in an armchair in front of the TV and seductively purr while I glide my hand down your hair or scratch you under your chin or behind your ears. Nor will you adorably watch me while I gently lay my head on your stretched belly, curing my headache and warming my face, and listening to your heartbeat and breathing mixed with quiet cooing. And no one will cut your whiskers because they are too long as, half joking and half serious, Grandma wanted to do while she was still alive....

*

No longer will you take me to your bowls of food. You will not wake up, yawn and stretch as much as you can before you crawl out from under the table. You will not give me that look of yours and seductively blink your big, warm eyes; and I will not drop what I was doing at that moment and approach you to cuddle you. You will not nod at me and coo before I touch you and narrow your eyes even more from sheer pleasure and then go. You will no longer stop after a few steps and turn around to check that I am behind you and, satisfied, carry on with your tail slightly raised after you assured yourself I am following you. No longer you will stop right in front of your bowls and wait for me, and start eating only when I pat you, thus giving you permission to eat. I don't know why you made up that rule, but the only logical ex-planation is that it was you. Those were your decisions, procedures and ways, similar to others', but unique, original and unrepeatable, just as you are.

The more I get into the depth of your character and dive into the sea of kindness with which you abound, the harder for me is everything I have done to sin against you. Everything I denied you.

Forgive me.

Forgive me. It was a beautiful day last week. I think it was Friday. The sun warmed like no other day of the year. There was a pleasant wind, and the scents of flowers and sprouted grass rose from the ground. I thought I would pick fresh green grass for you as soon as it grew a little more. I thought I'd surprise you with this gift. But I will never give it to you, love, and that makes me feel like garbage. If I had known. If I had only sensed—*if I had wanted to admit to myself!*—you could have tasted the first grass of this spring, no matter how short and unripe its leaves were. But I was a coward and ran from reality! I stole from you the last touch of just-awakened nature, because not even the trees had fully bloomed yet.

*

I sneak out again, cannot help myself. I escape to another room, blow my pain and bitterness into the already wet handkerchief before I return to you. Dad is still not there. He is hiding from you, us, reality, truth and death, while Mom is waiting for Saša. Minutes stand still. Everything stands still, including my hand that slides down your hair, gray, dark-brown, light-brown, with longer wisps on your belly, shorter, untidy and sprinkled with dandruff on your back, under your neck soft and aristocratic, once as fine as the best quality fur. My friends used to tease me they would be glad to wear your fur. If they saw you today, I think they would be ashamed of their own words, regardless of their being spoken in jest or how big a compliment they were to you back then.

You take a deep breath and, while exhaling, roll onto your back. Probably the last time you expose your belly to me; and, as in old days, I caress it with my fingertips. It is the last time we cuddle like this, and you know it. You give in to me completely, trying to remember my touch.

I remember it too, knowing this is the only physical contact I have with some living being, and that in few minutes I will lose it. I panic from the realization I won't be able to hug you again, feel your warm body on my hands, the tickling of your fur against my face. Fear builds in me from the emptiness I plunge into, and only the ringing in the stairwell saves me from bursting into tears, from which no one could tear me out.

Love, do not leave me!!!

You raise your head on standby, like a submarine periscope getting ready to surface. Who is ringing? Who is coming? You stretch your neck in anticipation. I am no longer interesting to you while I pet you on the top of your head and scratch under your grayish chin. Something else is happening now. Something new, something more important.

I absorb into my memory your big, yellow-green and somewhat tired eyes, knowing that a little longer, a little bit longer, and their flame will disappear. Although they will still be open, they will no longer watch me, nor will I see them. Never again....

You relax when you see Saša come. My poor old guy, you must be surprised by seeing him again in such a short time. If you only knew the reason for his arrival.... If you only knew about his mission as the angel of death....

Or, maybe you know why he's here? So you heroically await your destiny as you heroically endured all the pain and all the adversity that has befallen your languid body....

Saša, Mom and I, each from our own side, form a triangle of love in which we place you. True to himself, Dad is still hiding in the kitchen, looking for illusory comfort and drawing a non-existent strength from who knows which glass in a row. From the bag Saša takes and prepares two needles, comforting Mom and me. Mom is complaining that she doesn't have strength any more, that she lost three cats already (considering you the third loss). Saša listens to her attentively and expresses disbelief when he hears that after her return from London the veterinarians, in cold blood, told her that her Fanika was wrapped in a bag in a cage where they had put her after failed uterus surgery. Lulu, a big, yellow neighbor's cat, who fed at Mom's and her parents' place and visited them when they were still living in the city center, was killed by a car. And now it's your turn. Now it is time for you to leave her too. Mom is crying. I am also crying, but this time I don't look for a refuge by hiding in another room. I wipe my tears with my hand while Saša is trying to find a muscle in your left hind leg where he intends to give you the injection. Astonished, he finds only fur and flabby tissue because your illness has eaten everything else. The injection finally finds its way, and Saša explains what he gave you and what effect it will have on you. Not even five minutes have passed, and you, boosted by a supernatural power you got somewhere, abruptly push up on your front legs and vomit. Saša asks what is that white thing you ate, and I try to prevent you from jumping off the three-seater. Mom quickly returns from the bathroom with a paper towel on which you three times throw up pieces of undigested chicken. Before you calm down again, I see your indigo blue tongue. Love, you're sicker than I thought, and although I know the injections are bringing you much desired relief, I can't help but feel all the intensity of the pain you feel.

I lay you back down on the pillow and you relax. Your tummy rises and falls at more regular intervals. Saša talks. Explains. Usually it takes ten to fifteen minutes until the injection takes effect, but in your completely exhausted body, its effect is faster and almost everything happens in an instant. Saša and I sit with you, caressing you, and wait until you are fully asleep. Until you dream a dream from which you will not wake up. Or just fall asleep and forget about everything: illness, time, space, the injection you received, about all the beautiful and ugly goings on in your life, us who surround you, torn by indescribable pain and boundless love and who have become and were your family.

With the syringe needle Saša tests the reflexes on the

pads of your toes. He moves his hand in front of your eyes and checks whether you sleep. You are gone, love. You are completely unaware—of everything. He prepares a second injection and warns us that what is coming next is not nice and it might be better that we leave until he finishes. Mom is a little reluctant, but leaves. I'm staying. I had already decided that I would be with you until the very end, as I was determined when, a few days ago, I said in front of Mom, Dad and Saša that you should take your last trip from your home, from your bed. Although Saša mentioned the possibility of taking you to the clinic, I condemned my parents and myself to additional suffering. But it was the right thing to do. That was the last thing we could do for you for all the wonderful years you have given to us. And for which I will be thankful to you for the rest of my life.

Saša and I switch places because his shadow is disturbing him while he approaches you with the second injection. Once again he warns me it is an ugly scene. The injection will stay pinned in your body. But I want to know all that will happen and ask him whether he will give it to your heart. No, this injection which causes death is administered directly into the lungs and stops breathing. Asking him questions and listening to his answers, I don't notice when your lungs stopped moving. I also don't see Mom arrive. At about the same time Saša and I notice that you begin to urinate and Saša apologies for you, saying it happens to everyone when they die. As if he should apologize for you! Mom again jumps in with a paper towel by putting it under you.

It's over.

It is over....

You are not here anymore.

You're gone.

I do not know exactly when. And I do not know how. How I missed that moment. Which I dreaded. For so long. And which I've feared. That will tear us apart. And make us each go our separate ways.

Forever?!

*

Saša puts this syringe on the table as well and asks whether we have prepared a bag in which he will carry you.

I caress your motionless body and steal one more touch.

Saša says we did the right thing. Extending your life would be a real agony for you and there was a high probability you would die of suffocation. None of us wanted to put you through that, love, none of your angels of death.

I glance at the wall clock above the door. It is twenty past seven. I'm counting minutes backwards and estimating that you died about seven fifteen. From Mom I take a black garbage bag and unroll it while Saša is wrapping you in your blankets.

You're a little too big for them so the ball in which Saša rolled you opens. A breath of warmth that is leaving your body streams like a kiss down my hand when Saša puts you in the bag. You are so soft, so gentle, fragile, and beautiful. Saša closes the bag and I don't see you anymore....

We put the black bag into another one so it's easier

for Saša to carry you. I regret we didn't wrap you in one of your bigger blankets, but Saša says it isn't necessary. It's just your body in the bag. Saša also won't care what happens to his body when he dies, where they will put it. I agree with him. I'd prefer to be cremated too, and scattered in several places—in the rivers, deserts, on the glaciers, mountains and in savannahs, so no one knows where I rest. Closing you in the bag, he tells me to look after Mom and Dad and gestures towards the syringes for me to toss them in the trash.

Mom goes to the bathroom to throw in the toilet the paper towel on which you urinated and now settles accounts with Saša. We both know Saša doesn't charge for a full service when he tells the price. He takes money only for the costs of injections and remains consistent about that. We don't owe him anything else. It's not that we couldn't pay him; I believe he decided that because of you and because he loved you. Because of loving you, he went through this Calvary with us, and it will last for him while he carries you. Until you become ashes and turn into the dust from which you came.

On leaving, he finds strength once again to

encourage us. Sometimes the animals are so sick they walk on the edge of the abyss, but they don't have strength to jump into it. They wait for us to push them over the edge and for that they are grateful. Little one, I hope your fall wasn't painful.

What happens next is a little chaotic. I don't know who exactly does what, when Dad comes out of the kitchen and where he disappears after that, through which tunnels and catacombs Mom walks. I wander from room to hall to another room and back, confused and with red eyes from crying, knowing I must catch another look at the blue bag at the tram stop. From the corner of my eye and completely by accident I see two syringes on a table in the living room, neatly placed next to one another. I grab them while no one is around and take them to my room. I hide them in the drawer of my desk on which my computer is seated. Then I go out to the balcony and spot Saša. Instead of waiting at the tram stop, he is going on foot down our side of the street. Carrying the blue bag in his right hand.

With a light step, bowed head and stoop-shouldered, he makes his way through the parked cars and the street crowded with bulky waste. The garbage workers still haven't taken it away. How ironic. You are leaving on the day when the tenants in the street are disposing of the unnecessary things they have piled up in their basements and attics. They discard things they no longer want and need, and I have to throw away what I love so much and without which I do not want to live. You.

Reaching the Exit Theater, he has to get off the sidewalk and step on the tram tracks because going through the waste and stacked cars is impossible. This is the last time I see you. The day is paler and the evening darker, and several clouds traveling over this part of Zagreb grow darker and sadder. I stand on the balcony. My heart wants to tear my chest and jump out of it. Tears are streaming down my face. As if the sky sympathizes with me, it lets from the cloud a few drops which drizzle on my face. A light rain starts. Silent, light and rare.

Mom joins me, and the two of us stay a little longer on the balcony, looking in the direction in which you left. We conclude that Saša has to carry you in the rain, and he doesn't even have an umbrella. It is only when we go back to the room that the reality lifts its blade and swings it over our heads.

Drowning his pain, Dad drinks a glass too many and stumbles to bed. Soon after, a burst of sobs comes from the room. When Mom goes to comfort him, he chases her away, saying we have ruined his life and to leave him alone.

*

Mom sits in front of the television with a hypnotized look on her face, trying to follow a program with me. In fact, both of us sit like logs, not knowing where to go or what to do with ourselves. Now I'm choking, she says, placing her hand on her chest, and I don't know what to answer to her. I remember Saša's words—to look after Mom and Dad—and wonder how. How, Saša, when I am barely alive? The pain gains a new dimension, and, as the hours pass, it escalates to proportions which drive me to madness.

Mom and I start to talk. We talk about you. I tell her that the second injection didn't look as bad as Saša was saying, but, rather, the first one. The first injection was the one that determined your fate; the second only ended what had already started. Mom says it is hard for her to talk about you even with me, so only tomorrow will she phone uncle and others. Everything melts, sways, moves and disappears in the rebellion of emotions.

I killed you!!! Although I didn't give you the injections myself, but Saša did it, he was only the executor of my decision. Though my parents arranged everything with Saša before I came home, somehow we knew the last word would be mine, that I would be the one to decide how many days, hours, minutes you would have left. I brought you home fourteen years, eight months and twenty-seven days ago. I decided that after fourteen years, eight months and twenty-seven days you would leave your home. I killed you, and I don't want to seek justification in the words *putting down* and *euthanasia*! To hell with embellishing! I killed you, I, your angel of death. I took your life just as I gave it to you once, putting before my parents and grandmother a fait accompli they had to accept you in our home. What to call someone who kills a loved one, even only out of mercy???

My life, I am breaking down and rejecting you, and this evening has no end. It is so long. So painfully far the dawning is....

Thinking I have the strength, I go to my room and search for the button on my cell with Snježana's number. She will be the first person I will tell you are no longer with us. I'll ask her to let the others know, because I'm not sure I will have the nerve for another call. I can't even send the e-mails about your death. For two days already I've had problems with my computer and I can't log on the Internet today. Everything goes wrong tonight....

Snježana answers with a cheerful voice, but deep breathing and silence from my end. She repeats my name, and somehow I squeeze between breaths, It's not good. Marcel.... Marcel is gone.... And I crack like a century-old glacier, fractured by global warming. I blubber and choke in tears, pain and humiliation, but I am relieved for calling her. Snješko..., I say, and with someone else's voice distorted by crying, I tell her about you.

The pain in my head is so strong that I can't sleep a wink. This time it isn't a migraine. Or maybe it is, but increased with another pain that pulses with internal pressure as if my head will burst. I am clogged up with tears, and I feel as though I am sinking to the bottom of the sea. With each new foot death is approaching, but it doesn't bring me relief; instead the pain is intensifying to the point of being unbearable. What is the level of tolerance? Where are the limits of human endurance?

I toss and turn in bed. One moment I'm sweating and the next uncovering myself. Then I cover myself with a quilt all the way to my chin. I'm cold, very cold, even though temperatures are much higher these days and there's no reason for me to be so cold. No, this coldness is not climate caused. My body moans and weakens from lack of sleep and fatigue, whipped by pain.

With the sleeve of my pajamas I wipe my eyes and I turn my back to the window, irritated by the orange light of the street lamps. My eyelashes are sticky with tears and I blink through them at the empty space under the table where you lay this morning. My brain projects your outlines and, for a moment, I materialize you. I blink my eyes and you're gone again. The illusion melts and soaks into a pillow. Once more I call you to reality, but I'm suffocating, fighting for air like you. I hold onto that little sanity on this frenzied carousel of emotions.

*

I'm thankful for people like Snježana, who understand this kind of pain, because by some miracle they have evolved above the mediocrity of this world. Today I called no one else. I will leave everything for tomorrow because tomorrow is a new day. When I go out, when I go among the predators of my kind, it will be easier for me to hold back and conceal my grief. Then it will be easier to talk to others and send e-mails about your death to my friends and respond to text messages of condolence that will arrive during the day. I cannot cry anymore, love. I mean, I can. I have enough tears stored in me and I could cry until dehydration, but I am tired. My body trembles, my head is splitting, and for days I have felt a latent pain in my chest. I am fragile and crushed, like the millennial parchment carried by an eagle in his talons.

*

The dream refuses to give me forgiveness. I won't be granted mercy. I stay awake in agony while minutes tick by into the future.

Where are you now, doll? Does your body still exist as I remember it, or is it scattered in ashes and flying with smoke, free to the open skies? Are the traces of your existence already erased or will you disappear only the next day? I don't know in which hour you materialized in this world. I also don't know when you left it. Maybe Saša will tell us one day, but is that so important? Will that change a thing?

The emptiness will remain unfilled.

I don't know where people draw the strength to cope with such a loss. I don't know where Snježana finds the strength to cope with her losses. In four years she lost five of your brothers and sisters, but she is persistent in carrying and watching out for those who remain. Jelena survived disease, bullets, being under the wheels, poisons, crazy neighbors, but she still takes care of her animal kingdom, while Anita has a few small graves in the house yard in Berlin.

Your grave doesn't exist. You will never have it. You will stay buried in me. Mom and Dad will also carry you in their memory. And wherever I go, whatever I do, I will try to let you also feel a touch of the world through which we will walk together. I'll be your eyes. My heart will beat for you. My lungs will soak up the scents of the seasons, and the music from the radio will lull us to sleep together.

And I will tell people about you. Face to face, but also with this monument, whose construction with every click on the keyboard is nearing its end. My fingers are swollen from rapid typing. They slide and miss the keys from the strength of the strokes and then they return again. My hands and strokes are heavier and heavier from cramps, while tears, instead of sweat, wash the dust of carved emotions off my face. I will also tell them with the photographs you've left behind, this pathetic sentimentality before which I buckle, letting it enslave me. And I will be a happy slave, because I am a slave to something beautiful, to someone I love.

Now I stand even stronger in my assurance to spend the rest of my life helping and fighting for others. For those like you. This is the meaning that fills me, my motivating force (we can call it love, we can call it thirst for justice), until a rule of one law on this planet applies to everyone. I spend myself and will spend myself until the end, in order for every one of us to win the right to our own life. To life in which no one will exploit and oppress anybody, with no suffering, pain, fear. The right to live and not to be killed, tortured or abused in the name of the *higher purpose*, with no one asking us beforehand do we agree with that. The intellectual superiority and developed, modern, mechanized killing systems are not a cover for the crimes that my species commits on others, every moment, including this one, everywhere on our amazing, haunted planet of death. No excuse. There is just no excuse.

I don't know how much time is left for me, but the time I have been given will be devoted to you. All the good deeds I do, I will do in your name. Living with hope they will be worthy of what you did, enriching our life to the full. Our cup runneth over.

Thank you for being part of my life. Thank you for letting me be a part of your life. I am proud to have known you, my friend.

Morning dawns beautiful and sunny, but also with a fatigue the dream failed to remedy. I unmake a bed and open the door of the balcony; the family of pigeons is already sitting obediently on the railing, waiting for seeds and breadcrumbs for breakfast. Their number varies from morning to morning; sometimes there are seven, at times even twelve, and this morning I count nine. They are faithfully lined up on the balcony railing, our guard of honor.

I shake my head no to Mom's question whether I slept better last night and shut myself in the bathroom. I turn on the shower and, while shampooing my hair, I think about taking the hygiene litter you didn't use to Snježana for her cats. Emotions overflow me again and the sight of an unopened bag I bought you two days ago brings tears to my eyes. I sob in the shower while the pleasant, warm water washes my face and eyes, red from crying and shampoo.

I spend a minute drying my hair, dress and drink cocoa with soy milk. This morning, too, I cannot eat anything. The last meal I ate yesterday just after noon was a potato strudel for five Kunas. That's all I've eaten in the last nineteen hours. My stomach clenches at the thought of food.

Getting ready to leave the house, I twitch at the crackling of the parquet in the room. I hope to hear your walk, expecting to see you when I turn around. But I see emptiness where it should be you. Endless emptiness. I'm not the only one. Mom also got up during the night, thinking she heard the tapping of your feet. What Dad feels, I can't tell. I haven't talked to him yet. The morning conversation he and Mom had was nonsensical, and I didn't join it. Still, I liked to hear it; anything is better than silence to which I submit myself. I don't have the energy to be strong. I can't pretend and that is why I am withdrawing into myself. That's why I avoid them. If I cannot be their rock and support, if I cannot look after them as Saša said, then I can at least try not to make it more difficult for them. So I suffer in silence and go out, hiding my pain, and I know I should stay and be with them. Open like a flower, not closed, but I cannot. It's not that I do not care for them and love them, but this is not our time. It will come in a day or two, a week or a month.

This is *your* time.

I wander around the apartment, heading for something, but forgetting what it was, so I go back. I stop to compose myself and quit playing the fool. If you recall, even though it was a long time ago, how you felt when you woke up after castration, when all your four legs buckled, and when you were crawling around the apartment dazed and drugged, then you can imagine how I feel now. The only difference is that a part of my brain is taken out, a part of my heart cut out.

I take the syringes from their hiding place and, without thinking, put them on the table in the bag in which Saša brought them. When I get back to the room Mom is watching them and she asks me whether to throw them away. I tell her to leave them alone and check the e-mails that arrived overnight. When she leaves the room, with a quick move I put them in my front backpack pocket, but I change my mind and put them in the pocket on the left leg of my cargo pants. They are safer there. Less likely that someone will find them there or that I will lose them if I keep them with me.

It may sound bizarre that the tool with which I killed you I carry with me. That's all I have left of you. This is the last thing you felt, and that's why I want to keep them. Maybe I will throw them later, but now these emptied syringes are the most palpable thing that binds me to you. When Saša took you away last night, Mom immediately got to work and removed and cleaned your bowls for food, and then the boxes with your toilets. The green pillow with playful blue dogs was away before I even noticed it happening while the blanket on which you slept under the table in my room ended up airing on the courtyard balcony.

I help Mom collect the newspapers spread on the parquet to protect them in case you did not get to the toilet and peed on the floor instead. Only two nights ago Mom told me she found you in the morning with your front legs standing on the newspapers and gallantly dropping a load on the parquet. You would be surprised how many newspapers we have collected, together with the other old paper which is now in a bag I will empty this morning before I go to work.

When I come back, I'll tell Mom to give me your pillow. I want it near me. I won't ask for your blanket. It would be a little too much. The episode with the syringes perplexed her enough.

I am not the first nor the last one to mourn, but this is my way of mourning. It's my way to deal with the pain and to feel you next to me. I couldn't care less what others will say or think! They didn't know you. They don't know what you meant in my world.

I'm ready for the first challenge after your departure. In the same T-shirt, pants, sweatshirt and sneakers I wore on the day you died, I stand with a backpack on my back at the apartment door. The syringes and my wallet are in the pocket on my leg. The statistical report which I have to give today to the financial agency is in my backpack.

I say 'bye to my old folks who have already taken out the steam cleaner; soon the vacuuming of your hair from the carpets, the washing, painting and varnishing of the ruined parquet will start. Removing more evidence of your existence. *Damn parquet. If you only ruined it all, but were still alive!!!*

With my right hand I lift from the floor in the corridor a yellow bag with the remains of your paper, close the door and without hurry descend from the fourth floor. I stop at the door of the stairs—will I change my mind or do I have the guts to continue?

I grab the door handle, and the glittering sun spotlights my face and evaporates tears from the corners of my eyes.

A recycling bin for the wastepaper is right next to the kiosk across the street. The bag which I hold in my hand is heavier than the one Saša took with him over twelve hours ago. I'm not crossing the street. I continue along the route he traveled yesterday, stoop-shouldered and with lowered head, carrying in his right hand his small cargo.

On the day you died I came to the twelfth page of the novel *The Vampire Armand* by Anne Rice. Though the book is promising, I haven't taken it in my hands since then. I wanted to watch *The Village* on DVD, but it still waits for me. The last film I watched a little over a month ago at the movies was *Walk the Line* with two Hollywood vegetarians, Joaquin Phoenix and Reese Witherspoon. The last CD I bought was the Oscar-winning original motion picture soundtrack of *Brokeback Mountain*. The last time I laughed was on the day of your death. That day I stayed too long in the association and spent less than two hours with you. Do you think I will forgive myself that?

*

The street was cleaned this morning. There's almost no trace of the bulky waste on the part where I walk and which blocked Saša's way yesterday. I saunter and think about the symbolism of our (Saša's and my) cargo. A few minutes after you fell asleep Saša said you were probably suffering from a tumor, too, because he felt something lumpy while he examined you. This was supposed to make it easier that we pushed you off the cliff, straight to death. But it provoked in me completely the opposite effect. It was even harder for me because you were a greater fighter than I thought. You endured your pain in silence, brave and without complaint, as no man could.

There is a green light at the traffic light and I cross the street. I drop my cargo into a recycling bin on the corner of Slovenska Street and Grada Mainza Street. Newspaper after newspaper. One pile after another.

More proof of your existence.

I fold the empty bag and put it in my backpack. I

take a cell phone that hangs around my neck. I turn it on and see you sleeping in the photo on my screen. Numb from pain I pick and dial Anita's number. It's time I tell her about you. My Swabian, my bro. My soulmate.

I keep walking while the phone rings. I continue to walk when Anita answers the phone and when I talk to her and when we're done talking. All the way to Gundulićeva Street, and further on. Toward the fulfillment of my vow, in search of the way by which I will meet you again.

Marcel, I swear....

To Marcel

(1991—2006)

I stand on the balcony, and three floors below me, with noise and shudders of the building, the traffic glides down the street. Carried by light drifts, the clouds float on the sky, promising rain. I watch Saša and you leaving, pushing your way through the illegally parked cars and bulky waste carried out by tenants because they no longer need it.

It is April 19.

I follow you as you are getting more distant and smaller, shaking from crying, with the body tired of life. Saša has to step on the street to bypass the waste and the cars parked on the sidewalk, and then I lose sight of you. Of the blue bag with yellow handles in which your still warm and curled up body slept. When after a few steps he returns to the sidewalk, I lose him, too.

I gather strength and make the final decision. I strain my thoughts and force my body to move.

I'm on the balcony. I move along its length, not stopping until the end, until I come to the railing. On the table I have left a will with clear instructions, so that animals are not deprived of their rights in case something goes wrong and my plan fails. On top of it I put your favorite photo and the syringes I won't need anymore.

Now I am free.

Now I live at last.

And I look the enemy in the eyes.

I challenge death to the last duel. Defying it with the strength, I wish to believe, of not-wasted life. My actions will speak for or against me. And one monument I built. Now completed, it will beautify life for someone. Some will grieve and cry, others may be enraged. Many won't understand. That's the way with people. Always.

I refuse to obey the rules as I did most of my life. I refuse to accept death as something natural, as something that has to happen. I do not acknowledge it but take things into my own hands.

I put my hands on the railing.

I sharpen my weakened eyesight and strain the vessels in my arms, every muscle in my body. My head hurts. Don't know if it's a migraine or too much sorrow. Saša is again in my sight.... *(It works!)* He appears unclear, like a Bedouin in a desert mirage, and now I see the bag he is still holding in his right hand!

I close my eyelids, only peeking through them as through a rifle sight or the opening in a bunker. I focus, and this time you're even closer, more clear!

My heart is racing. It wants to jump out of my throat as I exhale a whining sigh and tears of joy. *Viola, my love.*

I do not notice the traffic stopping below me, the driver coming out of the tram, the passengers following him or peeking out of the windows, the growing groups of passers-by looking up at all four sides of the crossing. Some of them make frantic calls from their cell phones, probably calling the police, ambulance or firefighters.

I take matters into my own hands and swing another leg over the railing. Holding tight, I lean my back on the metal. The wind is playing with my hair, T-shirt, and pants.

I smile as I see Saša and you coming closer. Raindrops wash away tears that feed my chapped lips and tickle my unshaven neck.

My friend, brother....

Shouts and gasps are unnecessary when I let go of the railing and reach out to you. Completely un-necessary. I do not die as I float in the air, peaceful. I defy death and take matters into my own hands.

And learn the secret.

I enter the parallel world.

I open my eyes and protect them with my hand from the blinding sun that mercilessly attacks the bed where I lie, trying to get me out of it.

Mom shows up at the door and asks if I am fine. I look like I have a headache.

No, I don't have a headache. It was just a bad dream. I rub my face and realize that my cheeks are wet with tears. Listening to Mom and Grandma talking to Dad about something in the living room, I ponder her question. I remember that I had lain down with a strong migraine, one of the strongest I can remember, mixed with some intense feeling of sadness and grief. I felt as though a piece of façade had broken off a building I was passing under and hit me on my head. Or as if I hit my head into something solid.

I blink my eyes, tormented by the persistent sun, and notice the details in the room. Everything is so—in place. The balcony door is wide open. The chirping of birds is coming through it, together with the almost inaudible sounds of traffic which, without pollution, flows down the street. Vehicles on solar energy shamelessly buzz by those driven by water, daring them. Today they do not have to draw the stored energy, emptying their batteries, but as soon as it gets cloudy and the first rain falls, things will change. The roles will be reversed.

The balcony railing is green from creepers. Blossoms of morning glory and clusters of clematis adorn it like jewels. Miniature roses, pansies, tulips, hyacinths, sunflowers and other flowers are planted in pots along the balcony like in a parade, creating an amazing explosion of colors and scents. The growing family of pigeons happily coos dotted on the railing and on the shelf.

Mom and Grandma are on their way out to get fresh fruit and vegetables, soy milk, seitan and legumes, and Dad is already waiting in a car. I call after them not to forget the smoked tofu and Bajadera chocolates—by all means Bajadera chocolates!—and think how everyone today radiates warmth and gentleness. As if they are full of energy, no trace of tiredness on them. Their faces simply sparkle!

I stretch slowly and lazily all the way and sit up in bed. A broad smile spills over my face when I look at the balcony door....

You are there, surrounded by the colors, looking at me curiously. Next to you is a hibiscus the size of a grown man with branches heavy with big red flowers. Behind you the pigeons adjust their feathers and coo to each other, happy that you have made a covenant of peace with them. Filling the air, insects compete with butter-flies in pollinating flowers.

I call you, overwhelmed with waves of unstoppable love, my chest filled with cozy warmth. You take a step or two and, with grace that only you own, walk up to my bed, bringing with you the smell of clean air without smog and blossomed linden which swells with health in the neighboring street. You sit down, and the long fur on your chest gleams in the colors of spring and the patterns of a wild cat. Mom must be right when she says you are most likely a cross between a cat and a fox!

Once again I call you quietly and you sniff the fingers of my outstretched hand. Overcome by a new wave of warmth I lean toward you and kiss your forehead. You blink your big eyes the color of ripe sunflowers and nuzzle your nose against mine. You kiss me.

You are in my arms. Purring with pure joy, loudly and tirelessly, as if you haven't seen me in—I don't know how long. As if you have so much to catch up. You are a really weird cat. And I wouldn't trade you for all the promises of the universe.

I stroke your hair, scratch you under your chin and behind your ears. Your outpourings of love intensify. It's all right, little one. Everything's fine.

Indeed, I say to myself. Everything's fine. All is well. Everything is as it should be.

To whom to be grateful, my beloved one?

ACKNOWLEDGEMENTS

My thanks go to Ozren Ćuk, Tihana Hren, Jelena Boromisa, and Anita Euschen for their comments. Thank you for pushing me off the cliff because I'm not sure I would have had the courage to jump into this literary challenge.

Thanks to Aleksandra Hampamer for her valuable remarks, to Goran Pavletić for making immortal everything in the Croatian edition of this book and to the Croatian Ministry of Culture for their trust.

Thanks to Sonja Kunović who began this story and Saša Dujanović who ended it.

Thanks to my parents Ksenija and Dubravko and all those who by their existence wrote these pages. I'll never be able to express with words how much you mean to me, nor will this life be enough to thank you for everything.

Thanks also to the pigeons who wake me every morning from the railing and The Winged, who here and there boldly walked into my room before returning among his feathered friends, reminding me that this was not just a dream. Unfortunately, he is no longer with us either....

It is my great hope and wish I did justice to each one of you on these pages. I tried to commit to my mind, as I committed it to my heart, every hour and every day I spent connected with you in this larger-than-life story. I apologize for possible mistakes and omissions; my mind was exposed to the avalanche of powerful emotions it was hard to cope with.

For the help with my English translation, I want to thank a small but amazing team of selfless individuals and professionals from Australia, the United States, the United Kingdom, Ireland, Italy and Puerto Rico, and Aldina Šćulac, Mirjana Ptiček and Irena Krčelić who were my great *home* support and encouragement in my international endeavors. Thanks to Philip Newey, Thomas Carley Jr. and Kath Middleton for their much appreciated help as editorial advisors and proofreaders. Thanks to Kristina Pepelko who helped me with my first query letters and website announcements. Thanks to Jonathan Hill for brushing my blurb to its final glaze and for many useful tips of an experienced indie writer. Thanks to Anita Euschen (again!), Bruna Rocha and Dario Cannizzaro for bearing with me through my formatting nightmare and for looking for and providing answers to my never-ending questions! Thanks to Angel Ramon Medina, founder of the Hybrid Nation, for patiently guiding me all the way through my self-publishing journey. Thanks to MG Wells, Victoria M. Patton, and Rebecca Gransden who, along with all those people mentioned above, were my moral support and balance when my mind was projecting distorted images of sanity.

Zach Singh is the author of the amazing photo of himself and Oswald I *had* to have on my cover (Thanks, Zach, for saying yes!), beautifully designed by Mario Kožar MKM Media. You guys painted the face to the soul of my novel.

And finally, thanks to the one for whom I wrote all this—thank you, Marcel.

SHARE WHAT YOU LOVE
(A NOTE FROM THE AUTHOR)

Writing this book was a question of survival, it was not an option or a choice. This story is personal and very important to me, so thank you for reading it.

If you liked my writing and enjoyed reading *A World Without Color*, please stay with me and visit my website where you can subscribe to my mailing list. While you are already there, feel free to check the books I have published in Croatian and those I am planning on publishing in English, or read my blog Muse. I am honored and overwhelmed by your much appreciated support.

www.bernardjan.com

There are also other ways to connect with me and follow me: Twitter, Goodreads, LinkedIn and Steemit. I'll be happy to see you there!

There is no greater joy than to share what you love with those who appreciate it.

Thank you!

BJ

REVIEWS

Please consider leaving an honest review at your favorite retailer. It doesn't have to be long. Even only a sentence or two would make a huge difference and it would be much appreciated.

Indie authors depend on you. You are the reason why we are still writing and publishing. Thank you for that. Thank you for sharing our stories.